SKJC
6-17ᵏᵗ

D1129830

Roberto Clemente

Jennifer Strand

abdopublishing.com

Published by Abdo Zoom™, PO Box 398166, Minneapolis, Minnesota 55439. Copyright © 2017 by Abdo Consulting Group, Inc. International copyrights reserved in all countries. No part of this book may be reproduced in any form without written permission from the publisher. Abdo Zoom™ is a trademark and logo of Abdo Consulting Group, Inc.

Printed in the United States of America, North Mankato, Minnesota
072016
092016

THIS BOOK CONTAINS RECYCLED MATERIALS

Cover Photo: AP Images
Interior Photos: AP Images, 1, 8, 9, 13, 14, 15, 19; Kenneth Wiedermann/iStockphoto, 4–5; B Bennett/Getty Images, 5; Corbis, 7; J. Spencer Jones/AP Images, 10; Focus On Sport/Getty Images, 11, 17; Harry Cabluck/AP Images, 16; Ray Howard/AP Images, 18

Editor: Emily Temple
Series Designer: Madeline Berger
Art Direction: Dorothy Toth

Publisher's Cataloging-in-Publication Data
Names: Strand, Jennifer, author.
Title: Roberto Clemente / by Jennifer Strand.
Description: Minneapolis, MN : Abdo Zoom, [2017] | Series: Trailblazing athletes
    | Includes bibliographical references and index.
Identifiers: LCCN 2016941525 | ISBN 9781680792539 (lib. bdg.) |
    ISBN 9781680794212 (ebook) | 9781680795103 (Read-to-me ebook)
Subjects: LCSH: Clemente, Roberto, 1934-1972--Juvenile literature. | Baseball
    Players--Puerto Rico--Biography--Juvenile literature. | Generosity--Juvenile
    literature.
Classification: DDC 796.357092 [B]--dc23
LC record available at http://lccn.loc.gov/2016941525

Table of Contents

Introduction

Roberto Clemente was from Puerto Rico. He played in Major League Baseball.

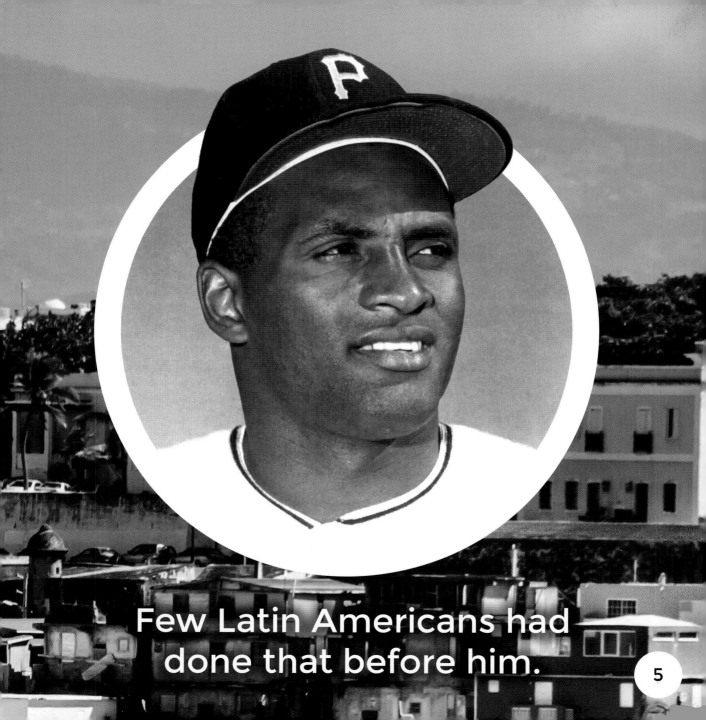

Few Latin Americans had done that before him.

Early Life

Roberto was born on August 18, 1934. He loved to play baseball. In high school he played for a **professional** team.

The Pittsburgh Pirates
drafted Clemente. He came to the
United States. He played right field.

Soon he was known
for his strong arm.

Clemente was also
a good hitter.

In 1960 his team won
the World Series.

History Maker

Life could be hard for Clemente.
Racism was common.
People treated him badly.

But he was proud of his heritage. He spoke against racism and worked to help others.

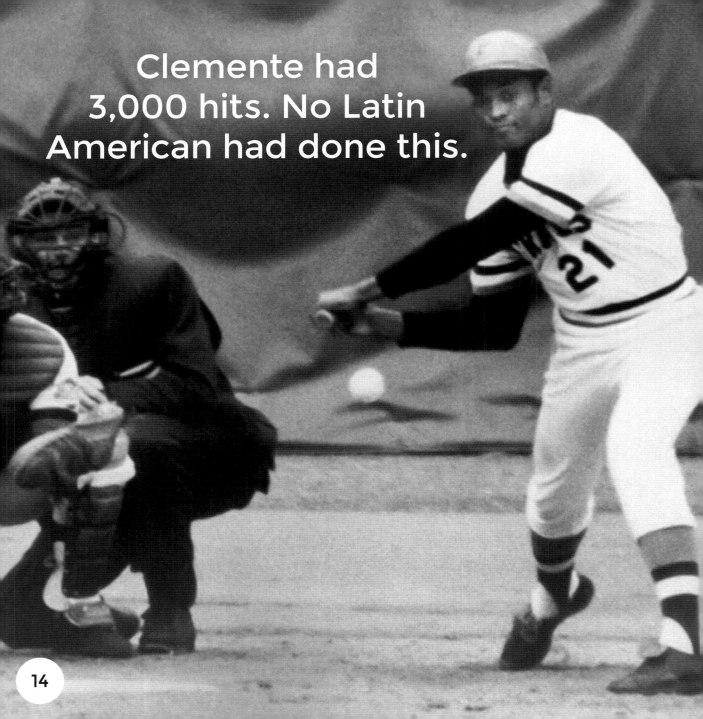

Clemente had 3,000 hits. No Latin American had done this.

He proved that he was one of
the best baseball players.

Legacy

On December 31, 1972, Clemente was in a plane crash. He died.

He was on his way to help
people after an earthquake.

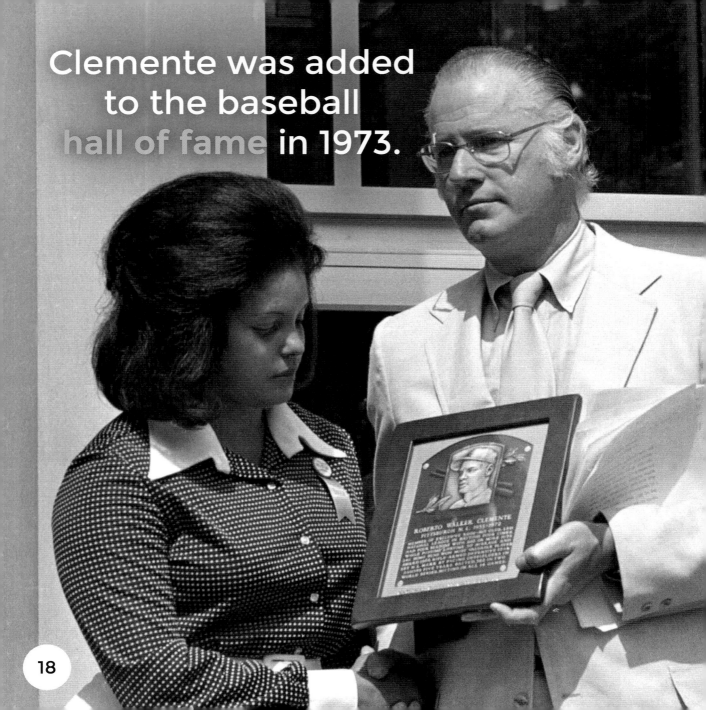

Clemente was added to the baseball hall of fame in 1973.

18

Players usually must wait five years after their last game. But Clemente was special. He was let in sooner.

Roberto Clemente

Born: August 18, 1934

Birthplace: Carolina, Puerto Rico

Sport: Baseball

Known For: Clemente was one of the first Latin Americans to play in Major League Baseball.

Died: December 31, 1972

Key  Dates

1934: Roberto Enrique Clemente Walker is born on August 18.

1955–1972: Clemente plays for the Pittsburgh Pirates.

1960: The Pittsburgh Pirates win the World Series.

1972: Clemente gets his 3,000th hit on September 30.

1972: Clemente is killed in a plane crash on December 31.

1973: Clemente is inducted into the National Baseball Hall of Fame.

Glossary

drafted - chose someone to play on a professional sports team.

hall of fame - a place that honors outstanding people from a sport.

heritage – the traditions, beliefs, and accomplishments of a country or group of people.

professional - paid to do something.

racism - treating someone poorly or taking away their rights because of the color of their skin.

Booklinks

For more information
on **Roberto Clemente**, please visit
booklinks.abdopublishing.com

Z⊙⊙m In on Biographies!

Learn even more with the Abdo Zoom
Biographies database. Check out
abdozoom.com for more information.

Index

24